RECLAIM YOUR DESTINY

31 DAY PROCLAMATIONS TO BUILD CHRIST ESTEEM AND GODLY SELF-IMAGE

LIFEWORK PRESS

RECLAIM YOUR DESTINY

31 DAY PROCLAMATIONS TO BUILD CHRIST ESTEEM AND GODLY SELF-IMAGE

GLORIA GODSON

LIFEWORK PRESS

RECLAIM YOUR DESTINY

31 Day Proclamations to Build Christ Esteem and Godly Self-Image.

LifeWork Ministries, Inc.
P. O. Box 56
Townsend, DE 19734

www.lifeworkministries.org
lifeworkministriesinc@gmail.com

LifeWork Press

© 2022 by Gloria Godson

All rights reserved solely by the author. No part of this book may be reproduced in any form without the permission of the author. For permission requests, contact [gloriagodson1@gmail.com].

Unless otherwise indicated, Scripture quotations taken from the Holy Bible, New Living Translation (NLT). Copyright ©1996, 2004, 2007 by Tyndale House Foundation. Used by permission of Tyndale House Publishers, Inc.

Scripture quotations taken from the New King James Version (NKJV)–*public domain.*

Printed in the United States of America.

ISBN: 978-9-9193-2137-6

Dedicated

To YOU

Men and Women of God who are fighting back and reclaiming your destiny in Christ!

TABLE OF CONTENTS

Introduction

Day 1— I AM A Child of God 1
Day 2— I AM Complete in Christ 3
Day 3—I AM the Righteousness of God 5
Day 4— I AM A New Creation in Christ 7
Day 5— I AM Loved By God..............................9
Day 6— I AM Royalty 11
Day 7 —I AM Precious To God 13
Day 8— I AM Known 15
Day 9 — I AM of Tremendous Worth and Value.....17
Day 10—I AM Free From People 19
Day 11— I AM the God Kind 21
Day 12— I AM Kept By God...............................23
Day 13— I AM Protected 25
Day 14— I AM Approved 27
Day 15— I AM A Winner 29
Day 16— I AM His Sheep and Hear His Voice.......31
Day 17— I AM Free from Guilt and Condemnation.33
Day 18— I AM Redeemed From Every Curse........35
Day 19—I AM Blessed 37
Day 20— I AM Fearless 39
Day 21— I AM Courageous 41

Day 22— I AM Strong 43
Day 23 —I AM A Warrior 45
Day 24— I AM Powerful 47
Day 25 — I AM Free From Bondage 49
Day 26—I AM Victorious Over the Devil 51
Day 27— I AM Supernaturally Favored 53
Day 28— I AM the Light Of The World.................55
Day 29— I AM God's Masterpiece 57
Day 30— I AM Healed 59
Day 31— I AM A Friend of God 61

Afterword..63

INTRODUCTION

A Christian who does not understand, embrace or walk in the reality of their identity in Christ will forfeit their destiny and the abundant life Jesus purchased for them on the cross; and instead, will live a life riddled with fear, defeat, sickness, poverty, mental and emotional bondage, and oppression.

Destiny is rooted in identity, and having your identity in Christ unlocks your divine destiny. When you know who you are in Christ, the devil can no longer intimidate, terrorize or bind you; sin can no longer be your master, and boss you around; chains that once held you captive have no option but to fall off, because you can no longer be bound; when you know, really know, believe, and appropriate the glorious truth of who you are in Christ!

Knowing who you are in Christ is the single most liberating and empowering truth a Christian can embrace. It positions you for divine destiny and sets you on the trajectory to overwhelming victory!

We have an enemy who wants to rob us of God's best for our lives. We live in a world that bombards us with negative voices, messages, and images specifically targeted to derail us, and stop us from living our lives according to God's design.

But God has given us His Word to light our path, show us the way, and keep us on course. The word of God, spoken in faith, is the most powerful weapon known to man. This book empowers you to boldly take hold of the word of God, mix it with faith in your heart, and launch it forth to achieve the plans and purposes of God for you and your family.

The proclamations in this book have been scripturally composed and specifically adapted to execute a dramatic self-redefinition that will forge a brand new destiny for you. They will challenge every voice speaking from your bloodline or human ancestry, revoke every legal right claimed by the devil to take you captive, break the power of demonic bondage and oppression in your life, and bring you out of captivity into divine destiny and purpose. These proclamations will help you to reclaim your divine destiny, and bring it into physical manifestation.

RECLAIM YOUR DESTINY

31 DAY PROCLAMATIONS TO BUILD CHRIST ESTEEM AND GODLY SELF-IMAGE

LIFEWORK PRESS

I AM A CHILD OF GOD

Scripture

For all who are led by the Spirit of God are children of God. So, you have not received a spirit that makes you fearful slaves. Instead, you received God's Spirit when he adopted you as his own children. Now we call him, "Abba, Father." For his Spirit joins with our spirit to affirm that we are God's children - Romans 8:14-17.

Proclamation

I AM a child of God! I am an offspring of God. In Him, I live and move and have my being. I am born again, by the incorruptible seed of the word of God. I am born into greatness. I am an heir of God and a joint heir with Christ. I have the DNA of Almighty God. I am a partaker of His divine nature. My identity is not in my possessions, performance, position, status, looks, or popularity. My identity is in Christ and Christ alone. I refuse to answer to any labels, limits or stereotypes that any man or woman may want to place on me. I break out of every box of human definition and limitation. I look the devil, sin, the world, and the flesh in the eye and declare, I BELONG TO GOD, and I answer to only one label, title and name – child of the Most-High God!

I AM COMPLETE IN CHRIST

Scripture

For in Christ lives all the fullness of God in a human body. So you also are complete through your union with Christ, who is the head over every ruler and authority – Colossians 2:10.

Proclamation

I AM complete in Christ! I am seated in heavenly places in Christ Jesus, far above every rule, authority, power, or dominion, not only in this world, but in the world to come. In Christ lives all the fullness of God in human form. He is the embodiment of all the attributes of God, and I am completely filled with God as Christ's fullness overflows within me. I am a God-carrying vessel, filled with the maximum load of God! I do not look outside of myself and Christ who lives in me, for my sense of self-worth, validation, confidence, affirmation, and wellbeing. I am self-sufficient in Christ's sufficiency. I do not look to anyone or anything else to complete me or make me happy. I am complete in Christ. In Him, I AM ENOUGH!

I AM THE RIGHTEOUSNESS OF GOD

Scripture

For He made Jesus who knew no sin *to be* sin for us, that we might become the righteousness of God in Him - 2 Corinthians 5:21.

Proclamation

I AM the righteousness of God in Christ! God made Jesus, the only one who never sinned, to become sin for me, so that I might become the righteousness of God through my union with Him. I receive and appropriate the righteousness of Christ. Sin is no longer my master! I put off my old sinful nature and my former way of life, and I put on my new nature, created to be like God, truly righteous and holy. I am righteous, and live righteously, according to my new nature, the nature of God in me. I reject and renounce all bitterness, lying, stealing, rage, anger, harsh words, and slander, as well as all types of evil behavior. Instead, I will be kind, tenderhearted, forgiving others, just as God through Christ has forgiven me. I AM the righteousness of God. I will not use foul or abusive language. I will not bring sorrow to God's Holy Spirit by the way I live.

I AM A NEW CREATION IN CHRIST

Scripture

Therefore, if anyone *is* in Christ, *he is* a new creation; old things have passed away; behold, all things have become new - 2 Corinthians 5:18.

Proclamation

I AM a new creation in Christ! Jesus Christ is my Lord and Savior. I am redeemed, not with mere silver or gold, which lose their value, but with the precious blood of Christ, the sinless, spotless, Lamb of God. In my spirit, I look exactly like Jesus because I am joined with Him. I celebrate my spiritual life and identity in Christ. I have God's Spirit, the Holy Spirit, living in me. I have a new heart, a heart that loves and treasures the word of God. I have spiritual ears, that hear what the Holy Spirit is saying. I have new eyes that see in the spirit. I have a new mind, the mind of Christ. In Jesus's name, I reject old patterns of thought, mindsets, strongholds, habits and sinful desires, and declare that I walk in newness of life. I take authority over every voice speaking against me from my past and human ancestry, and drown them with the voice of the blood of Jesus. I shut down every accusation from the devil. I walk in the light, as God is in the light; I have fellowship with Him, and Jesus' blood cleanses me of all sin.

_____

_____

_____

_____

_____

_____

_____

_____

_____

_____

_____

_____

_____

_____

_____

I AM LOVED BY GOD

Scripture

I have loved you, with an everlasting love. With unfailing love I have drawn you to myself - Jeremiah 31:3.

Proclamation

I AM loved by God with a lavish, extravagant, and everlasting love! God demonstrated His great love toward me, in that while I was still a sinner, Christ died for me. How deeply intimate and far-reaching is His love! How enduring and inclusive it is! Endless love beyond measurement that transcends my understanding. Unconditional love that knows no limitations, reservations, or obstacles. This love pours into me until I am filled to overflowing with the fullness of God! Today, I believe and receive the love of God; and declare that my roots grow down deep into His love and keep me strong. I have the power to understand how wide, how long, how high, and how deep His love is, and I am made complete with all the fullness of life and power that comes from God.

I AM ROYALTY

Scripture

But you are a chosen people, a royal priesthood, a holy nation, God's special possession, that you may declare the praises of him who called you out of darkness into his wonderful light -1 Peter 2:9.

Proclamation

I AM hand-picked, selected and chosen by Almighty God; I am His special treasure, I am royalty! God has made me a priest and a king in His kingdom. He called me out of darkness to experience His marvelous light, and He identified, announced and publicly acknowledged me as His very own. I belong to God and my identity flow from Him! My Father is the King of kings and Lord of Lords. The whole earth belongs to Him, and everything in it. He is the sovereign ruler of the universe. He has called me to showcase His glorious love, grace, power, and wonders throughout the world. I AM royalty! I, who at one time did not know God, has now become God's delight, a child of the King, a joyful recipient of God's grace, and drenched with His love and mercy. Once I had no identity as a person; now I am identified as a child of God. Hallelujah!

_____

_____

_____

_____

_____

_____

_____

_____

_____

_____

_____

_____

_____

_____

I AM PRECIOUS TO GOD

Scripture

Since you are precious and honored in my sight, and because I love you, I will give people in exchange for you, nations in exchange for your life - Isaiah 43:4.

Proclamation

I AM precious to God! God gave Jesus, the very best that heaven has for me. He believes in me, and empowers me to believe in myself. I am a person greatly beloved. Jesus gave His life for me, that is the measure of my worth and value. God is on my side. God is for me, He is not against me. No good thing will He withhold from me. God has blessed me and wants to be good to me. I am His beloved child in whom He is well pleased. God has released his omnipotent power and deployed His angels to watch over me and war on my behalf. He is with me, and will move heaven and earth to help me. I am more than a conqueror through Christ. God has made me prosperous in wealth and in health. I walk in abundance and overflow. I can do all things through Christ. God's plan is to give me and my family a good life and a great future.

_____

_____

_____

_____

_____

_____

_____

_____

_____

_____

_____

_____

_____

_____

I AM KNOWN

Scripture

Before I formed you in the womb, I knew you, and before you were born, I consecrated you - Jeremiah 1:5.

Proclamation

I AM deeply and intimately known by God! Lord, you examine my heart and know everything about me. You know when I sit down or stand up. You know my thoughts. You know everything I do. You know what I am going to say before I say it. You place your hand of blessing on my head. You are not embarrassed or disappointed by me. You know my failures, public and private, you know the things that make me cry, you know the things I am ashamed of, but you never reject me or diminish your attention toward me. You tenderly stroke my hair and count the hairs on my head. When I cry, you scrape every tear and save it in your bottle. You think about me all the time. Your thoughts about me are countless, like the sands on the seashore. There is no place so dark, so deep, so high or so far that you are not there. No place I can go, that you won't go with me. I do not want to be anywhere, do anything, or be with anyone that will distract me from your presence.

_____
_____
_____
_____
_____
_____
_____
_____
_____
_____
_____
_____
_____

I AM OF TREMENDOUS WORTH AND VALUE

Scripture

For you know that God paid a ransom to save you from the empty life you inherited from your ancestors. And it was not paid with mere gold or silver, which lose their value. It was the precious blood of Christ, the sinless, spotless Lamb of God – 1 Peter 1:18-19.

Proclamation

I HAVE tremendous worth and value! I am a child of Almighty God! My value comes from my source. It does not come from my performance, whether or not people like me, how much money I have, who I know, what I drive, how I look, or where I live. God is my source of origin, and that source will never diminish in value. I don't need to convince people of my value. Jesus already did that. I simply own my value. I will not discount myself or sell myself short. I will not waste my time with, or give myself to people who do not value me. God made me an original, I will not be a cheap copy. I am an uncommon package, with my temperament, personality, quirks, skin color, and ethnicity. I was uniquely put together by God. Nothing about me is an accident. I am one of a kind. Nothing and no one can truly devalue me, because my value comes from God. Jesus paid full price for me. I will not give myself away at a discount!

_____

_____

_____

_____

_____

_____

_____

_____

_____

_____

_____

_____

_____

_____

_____

I AM FREE FROM PEOPLE

Scripture

Jesus said, your approval means nothing to me. I do not accept the honor that comes from men - John 5:41.

Proclamation

I AM free from people, like Jesus was free from people! I do not look to people for approval, validation, acceptance or applause. I do not lean, rely on or draw my self-image or self- esteem from human opinion, good or bad. The approval of people cannot define, validate or confirm me, and their disapproval, rejection or ridicule cannot invalidate or genuinely diminish me. They are not God, so, their opinion doesn't matter and their approval is not needed! I renounce every need or craving for human approval. I have Almighty God's approval and His approval does not depend on my works, looks, performance, or people's expectations. People are fickle, but God is not. He is constant, and His approval is unwavering. In Jesus name, I inaugurate a fast from the praise, approval, or validation of people. I declare, that I AM free from the definitions, labels, stereotypes, opinions, affirmations or rejection of people, and the world!

_____
_____
_____
_____
_____
_____
_____
_____
_____
_____
_____
_____
_____

I AM THE GOD KIND

Scripture

Then God said, let us make human beings in our image, to be like us... So, God created human beings in his own image. In the image of God he created them; male and female he created them – Genesis 1:26-28.

Proclamation

I AM the Godkind! God reproduced me after His own kind. He made me only a little lower than Himself and crowned me with glory and honor. He put me in charge over everything He made, and put all things under my authority. I have His attributes and nature, and can manifest His power. I am His offspring! It is through him that I live and function and have my identity; my lineage comes from him. I look exactly like Jesus in my spirit. As He is, so am I in this world. I am the image of God. I know my identity in Christ and I walk in it. God has commissioned me to occupy and rule over the earth, acting in His stead. I will faithfully execute that assignment. I AM the god-kind. I say NO to sin, the world, my flesh and the devil. I say NO to sickness, poverty, calamity, bondage or limitation. I say YES to God's plan, presence, purpose, passion and power.

I AM KEPT BY GOD

Scripture

You are kept by the power of God through faith for salvation ready to be revealed in the last time - 1 Peter 1:5.

Proclamation

I AM kept by the power of God! I am upheld by the omnipotent hand of God. Thank you, Lord, for all the things I went through, that could have destroyed me; all the times I was down to nothing; all the times I wanted to give up, but was empowered to take another step; and all the times, when the devil had me in a corner and was coming in for the kill, BUT GOD intervened, just in the nick of time. I am kept by the power of God. The Lord is my keeper. As the mountains surround Jerusalem, so the Lord surrounds me. God has given His angels orders to keep me in all my ways. He will not allow my foot to slip or to be moved; He Who keeps me does not slumber. Yes, He who keeps me and my family will not slumber nor sleep. The Lord is my keeper; He is my shade on my right hand. The sun shall not smite me by day, nor the moon by night. The Lord will keep me from all evil; He will keep my life. The Lord will keep my going out and my coming in from this time forth and forevermore.

I AM PROTECTED

Scripture

The name of the LORD *is* a strong tower; the righteous run to it and are safe – Proverbs 18:10.

Proclamation

I AM protected! I dwell in the secret place of the Most High, I abide under the shadow of the Almighty. I declare that the LORD alone is my refuge, my place of safety; my God, and I trust Him. He rescues me from every trap and protects me from deadly disease. He covers me with His feathers, He shelters me with His wings. His faithful promises are my armor and protection. I am not afraid of the terrors of the night, nor the arrows that fly in the day. I do not dread the disease that stalks in darkness, nor the disaster that strikes at midday. Though a thousand fall at my side, and ten thousand are dying around me, these evils will not touch me. I just open my eyes, and see how the wicked are punished. Because I have made the LORD my refuge, and the Most High my shelter, no evil will conquer me; no plague will come near my home. God has ordered His angels to protect me and minister to me wherever I go. The LORD rescues and protects me who trust in His name.

_____

_____

_____

_____

_____

_____

_____

_____

_____

_____

_____

_____

_____

_____

_____

I AM APPROVED

Scripture

Everyone who believes has God's approval through Faith in Jesus Christ – Romans 3:22.

Proclamation

I AM accepted and approved! Almighty God has approved of me! He approved of me before anybody else had a chance to disapprove, and His approval is unconditional and unwavering. I recognize that not everyone will understand, support or approve of me, and that is okay. I have God's approval! My heavenly Father has selected, affirmed and confirmed his love, blessing and favor on me. It doesn't matter who does not accept or approve of me. God is for me, who can be against me? The Creator of heaven and earth has determined to stand with me, tell me, who could ever stand against me? God's approval empowers me! God's favor will take me to new heights, open new doors for me, position me for increase, elevate me, announce me and move me to new levels of influence! In Christ, I AM enough! I am good enough, smart enough, strong enough, and attractive enough. In Christ, I AM Enough!

I AM A WINNER

Scripture

The LORD will make you the head and not the tail, and you will always be on top and never at the bottom – Deuteronomy 28:13.

Proclamation

I AM a winner! I have strength for all things in Christ. I am ready for anything and equal to anything through Christ who infuses inner strength into me; I am self-sufficient in Christ's sufficiency. I am anointed to prosper and empowered to succeed. I have the spirit of excellence, a winner's attitude and great work ethic! I am motivated, confident, and driven to manifest all the excellencies of God. I call forth into my life all the human, material, financial and relational resources that I need to fully accomplish God's plan and purpose for my life. I am physically, mentally, and emotionally ready for the new things God has planned for me. My steps are ordered and directed by the Lord. I am starting over, with a new thought pattern, positive emotions, strong connection to the Lord, and a new faith and confidence in myself. God will not allow anyone to derail me or keep me from destiny. In every challenge and situation, overwhelming victory is mine through Christ, who loves me.

___

___

___

___

___

___

___

___

___

___

___

___

___

___

___

___

I AM HIS SHEEP AND HEAR HIS VOICE

Scripture

My sheep listen to my voice; I know them, and they follow me – John 10:27.

Proclamation

I AM His sheep and I hear His voice! Lord Jesus, I hear your voice and follow you joyfully. I have a discerning ear. I hear your voice through your word, through prayer, and the Holy Spirit who lives in me. I am willing and obedient to your instructions. I am a doer of the word and not a hearer only. My life is in alignment with Your plan and purpose. I AM your sheep and I do recognize your voice. I will never be lost and no one can snatch me out of your hands. A stranger's voice I will not hear. I will not listen to seducing spirits or doctrines of devils. I will not listen to the voice of the accuser, shame, anxiety, fear, and reproach. I will not listen to the voice of the world system, or my sinful desires. Rather, I hear the voice of God saying, "this is the way, walk in it". Thank you,

Lord, that you have given me the tongue of a disciple; that I should know how to speak the right words, at the right time, to the right people. You wake me up, every morning, and cause me to hear as a disciple.

I AM FREE FROM GUILT AND CONDEMNATION

Scripture

There is therefore now no condemnation to those who are in Christ Jesus, who do not walk according to the flesh, but according to the Spirit - Romans 8:1.

Proclamation

I AM free from guilt and condemnation! God has justified me! To Him, it is just as if I had never sinned. There is no condemnation for me because I belong to Christ. I proclaim Tetelestai! My sin debt is PAID IN FULL!!! Jesus paid for my every sin, infraction, iniquity and transgression, and has set me free. I reject the lies and accusations of the devil. I am the elect of God, holy and beloved! Who can bring any charge against me, since God Himself has justified me? God has given me right standing with Himself, who then will condemn me? My conscience is clean and clear, and I walk in the glorious liberty of the children of God. I AM free and empowered to make better, healthier and more biblical choices and decisions. I take my joy, peace, happiness, and freedom back. Every voice that rises up against me in judgement, I condemn!

_____

_____

_____

_____

_____

_____

_____

_____

_____

_____

_____

_____

_____

_____

_____

_____

I AM REDEEMED FROM EVERY CURSE

Scripture

But Christ has rescued us from the curse pronounced by the law. When he was hung on the cross, he took upon himself the curse for our wrongdoing. For it is written in the Scriptures, "Cursed is everyone who is hung on a tree – Galatians 3:13.

Proclamation

I AM free from every curse! Jesus has delivered me from the curse pronounced by the law. When He hung on the cross, He took upon Himself the curse for my wrongdoing. He canceled the record of all charges against me and nailed it to His cross. He disarmed powers, principalities, the spiritual rulers and authorities and shamed them publicly by His victory over them on the cross. I reject, renounce, cancel, terminate, and overthrow every curse, hex, omen, spell, generational curse, or satanic covenant operating in my life and family. I bind, demolish and obliterate every witchcraft, divination, incantation or magic spells against me and my family. I shut down the operation of every wicked spirit supervising and enforcing any curse, dysfunction or bondage in my life and family. Jesus has set me free, and I am free indeed. I am blessed, I cannot be cursed. My blessing is irreversible. I have the blessings of Abraham.

I AM BLESSED

Scripture

All praise to God, the Father of our Lord Jesus Christ, who has blessed us with every spiritual blessing in the heavenly realms because we are united with Christ - Ephesians 1:3.

Proclamation

I AM blessed, prosperous, strong, favored, successful, productive, vigorous, fruitful, and wealthy! All the blessings of God pursue and overtake me. I am blessed in the city and blessed in the suburbs, blessed going out and blessed coming in. I am blessed in my mind, will and emotions. I walk in abundance, increase and overflow. I am blessed physically, spiritually, financially, socially, intellectually, relationally, and influentially. My cup overflows! My children, family, and I are blessed. Wherever we go and whatever we do, we are supernaturally blessed. The LORD has commanded a guaranteed blessing on our lives. We stand under open heavens. We will lend to many, but will not need to borrow. The LORD has made us the head and not the tail, always on top and never at the bottom. We are empowered to succeed and anointed to prosper. God's covenant of blessing, favor, grace and peace will never be broken in our lives.

___
___
___
___
___
___
___
___
___
___
___
___
___

I AM FEARLESS

Scripture

For God has not given us a spirit of fear and timidity, but of power, love, and self-discipline – 2 Timothy 1:7.

Proclamation

I AM fearless! God has not given me a spirit of fear, but of power, love, and sound mind. I say NO to fear in all its forms. I reject every spirit of bondage to fear. God is my refuge and strength, my very present help in trouble, so, I will not fear. The LORD is my light and my salvation, so whom shall I fear? The Lord is my fortress, protecting me from danger, so why should I fear or tremble? The LORD is for me, I will not fear, what can mere people do to me? God Himself has said, that He will not in any way fail me, nor give me up, nor leave me without support. He will never leave me helpless, or forsake me, or let me down, or relax His hold on me! So, I take comfort and I am encouraged and I confidently and boldly say, the

Lord is my Helper; I will not panic, fear, worry or be terrified. What can man do to me? Hallelujah! I have no fear, for the Lord is with me. I am not discouraged, for the Lord is my God. He strengthens, helps and upholds me with His victorious right hand.

_____
_____
_____
_____
_____
_____
_____
_____
_____
_____
_____
_____
_____
_____
_____
_____

I AM COURAGEOUS

Scripture

This is my command, be strong and courageous! Do not be afraid or discouraged. For the LORD your God is with you wherever you go - Joshua 1:9.

Proclamation

I AM bold and courageous! The Lord, my God is with me. Because He is at my right hand, I shall not be moved. I am not discouraged. I am steadfast, firm, and immovable. My heart is fixed, trusting in the Lord. The Lord Himself goes before me and is with me, I am never alone. I am on my guard; I stand firm in faith; I am courageous, and I am strong! In God I have put my trust and confidently take refuge; I shall never be put to shame or confusion! The Lord has strengthened my hands for war and my fingers to fight. I take a stand for righteousness, and speak up in the name of the Lord. I am a bold witness for Christ, and a courageous soldier of the cross. I do not cast away my confidence in God, which has a

great reward. I know that the battle is not mine, the battle is the Lord's. He will fight for me, and I will hold my peace. With God's help I will fight like a hero, for He has trampled down my enemies.

I AM STRONG

Scripture

Be strong in the Lord and in his mighty power – Ephesians 6:10.

Proclamation

I AM strong in the Lord and in His mighty power! God has unleashed within me the unlimited riches of His glory and favor. His supernatural strength floods my innermost being with His divine might and explosive power! The Lord is on my side, He is among those who help me, therefore I know that I will triumph over all my enemies. It is better to trust and take refuge in the Lord than to put confidence in man. It is better to trust and take refuge in the Lord than to put confidence in princes. My enemies surrounded me to attack me, but in the name of the Lord I have cut them off! They surrounded me on every side; but in the name of the Lord I have cut them off! You, my adversary, thrust sorely at me that I might fall, but the Lord helped me. The Lord is my Strength and Song;

and He has become my Salvation. Shouts of rejoicing are in my home. The Lord has done for me great things. The right hand of the Lord does valiantly and achieves strength! The right hand of the Lord is exalted. I shall not die but live, and declare the works of the Lord.

I AM A WARRIOR

Scripture

We are human, but we don't wage war as humans do. We use God's mighty weapons, not worldly weapons, to knock down the strongholds of human reasoning and to destroy false arguments – 2 Corinthians 10:3-4.

Proclamation

I AM a warrior for Christ! I am a soldier of the cross. I am not fighting against flesh-and-blood enemies, but against evil rulers, authorities, cosmic powers of darkness, and spiritual forces in the heavens. I stand strong and victorious with the force of Christ's explosive power flowing in and through me. I put on God's complete set of armor, so I am protected as I fight against the evil strategies of the devil! I put on truth as a belt to strengthen me, and righteousness as the protective armor that covers my heart. I stand on my feet alert, always ready to share the gospel of peace. In every battle, I take faith as my wrap-around shield, to extinguish the blazing arrows of the evil one! I put on the knowledge of who I am in Christ as a helmet to protect my thoughts from Satan's lies. I take the mighty, razor-sharp, sword of the Spirit, the spoken Word of God, and pray passionately in the Spirit. Thanks be to God for the victory in Christ!

I AM POWERFUL

Scripture

For the kingdom of God is not just a lot of talk, it is living by God's power - 1 Corinthians 4:20.

Proclamation

I AM Powerful! I have supernatural power. God's mighty power is at work in me to accomplish great things. Living in me is Christ who floods me with his glorious, inexhaustible power! I am a body wholly filled and flooded with God Himself! Embedded within me, is a heavenly treasure chest filled with the riches of God's glory, power, might, authority, dominion and excellence. God's miraculous power constantly energizes me. The same mighty power that raised Jesus from the dead, lives inside of me. This limitless, unstoppable power of Almighty God is working mightily in me. Jesus has given me power and authority over all the power of the devil. I take the limits off! I choose to believe for great things.

Eyes have not seen, ears have not heard, and no mind has imagined what God has prepared for me. I believe, receive and appropriate them today. God's power in me, will achieve infinitely more than my greatest request, my most unbelievable dream, and exceed my wildest imagination!

I AM FREE FROM BONDAGE

Scripture

So Christ has truly set us free. Now make sure that you stay free, and don't get tied up again with a yoke of bondage – Galatians 5:1.

Proclamation

I AM free from bondage! Jesus Christ has set me free, and I am free indeed. I take authority over depression, and declare that I am far from oppression, it shall not come near me. I live in peace and freedom from terror. No weapon formed against me shall prosper, and every tongue that rises against me in judgement, I condemn. I cancel every plan of the devil to steal, kill or destroy in my life! The law of the Spirit of life in Christ Jesus, has set me free from the law of sin and death. I am free from oppression, bondage, calamity, death and affliction. Christ has set me free to live a free life, I refuse to be entangled again in a yoke of bondage. So, I take my stand! Never again will I let anyone put a harness of slavery on me. I have the Holy Spirit living inside of me, and where the Spirit of the Lord is, there is freedom. Jesus has set me free, and I choose to walk in the glorious freedom that belongs to the children of God.

_____

_____

_____

_____

_____

_____

_____

_____

_____

_____

_____

_____

_____

_____

_____

I AM VICTORIOUS OVER THE DEVIL

Scripture

You are of God, little children, and have overcome them, because He who is in you is greater than he who is in the world - 1 John 4:4.

Proclamation

I AM victorious! I belong to God and have conquered the devil and his demons. Jesus who lives in me is far greater than the devil and his agents who are in the world. On the cross, Jesus vanquished the devil, canceled the record of the charges against me and nailed it to the cross. He disarmed the spiritual rulers and authorities, and shamed them publicly. All my sins are forgiven, my slate is wiped clean, my old arrest warrant is canceled and nailed to Christ's cross. Anything the devil is trying to do in my life and family today cannot be done because of what Jesus already did on the cross 2000 years ago. Jesus's work is finished, complete, lavish, total, and eternal. I cannot be bound, poor, sick, fail, or be oppressed because Jesus has already healed, saved, delivered, and set me free. I am blessed; I cannot be cursed; I am healed; I cannot be sick; I am free; I cannot be bound; I am rich; I cannot be poor. I cannot be cursed, yoked, or defeated because of what Jesus did for me on the cross. I stand in all the finished works of Christ.

I AM SUPERNATURALLY FAVORED

Scripture

You have found favor, loving-kindness, and mercy in My sight and I know you personally and by name - Exodus 33:17.

Proclamation

I AM supernaturally favored! I have found favor in the sight of God, and He knows me by name. He has blessed me and surrounded me with His favor as a shield. The time for the manifestation of God's supernatural favor in my life, the appointed time, has come, and it is NOW! God's favor has set me apart, elevated me, announced me and positioned me. I have favor and good success in the sight of God and man. Goodness and mercy pursues me and overtakes me, all the days of my life. God has set a table before me in the presence of my enemies! He has anointed my head with oil, and my cup overflows! God's favor is working mightily in my life, opening doors, and making a way. His favor is for my entire lifetime. The night of weeping is over and joy has come this morning. Like Esther won favor and grace in the eyes of the king, I have received supernatural favor, grace, and honor; and God has set the royal crown of distinction, excellence and glory upon me. Like Jesus, I increase daily in wisdom, stature and favor with God and man.

I AM THE LIGHT OF THE WORLD

Scripture

"You are the light of the world, like a city on a hilltop that cannot be hidden - Matthew 5:14.

Proclamation

I AM the light of the world! Because Jesus lives in me, I have the light of life. I am like a city on a hilltop that cannot be hidden. My life is on display, like a letter skillfully crafted by God's hand for all to read. My light shines brightly and illuminates my world and sphere of influence. People who don't know God, can see Him in and through me. I will not hide my light, but will let it shine brightly before others so that everyone will see it and praise my heavenly Father. My light shines in the darkness, and the darkness can never extinguish it. God is light, and in Him is no darkness at all. As I walk with Him, I am flooded with and reflect His light, and the blood of Jesus continually cleanses me from all sin. God's shining light guides me in my daily choices and decisions; and the revelation of His word makes my pathway clear. I walk in the highway of light, and my path shines brighter and brighter until the full light of day. I declare that light overtakes darkness in every area of my life.

_____

_____

_____

_____

_____

_____

_____

_____

_____

_____

_____

_____

_____

I AM GOD'S MASTERPIECE

Scripture

For we are God's masterpiece. He has created us anew in Christ Jesus, so we can do the good things he planned for us long ago - Ephesians 2:10.

Proclamation

I AM God's masterpiece! I see myself strong, healthy, talented, powerful, victorious, and living the abundant life Jesus purchased for me. I am God's expert workmanship, His work of art, created in Christ Jesus, reborn from above, spiritually transformed, renewed, and ready to be used for good works, which God prepared for me beforehand. I choose to walk in obedience and take the paths which God set, so that I would live the good life which He prearranged and made ready for me. God made all the delicate, inner parts of my body, and knit me together in my mother's womb. I am fearfully and wonderfully made. He saw me before I was born and every day of my life is recorded in His book. I go forth today to do the good works He has planned for me to do – to manifest His goodness and glory; to speak life instead of death, order instead of chaos, victory instead of defeat, mercy instead of judgement, love instead of the law. I am God's masterpiece and will fulfill His divine design for my life.

_____

_____

_____

_____

_____

_____

_____

_____

_____

_____

_____

_____

_____

_____

I AM HEALED

Scripture

He personally carried our sins in his body on the cross so that we can be dead to sin and live for what is right. By his wounds you are healed - 1 Peter 2:24.

Proclamation

I AM healed by the stripes of Jesus! I am healthy and whole, nothing missing, nothing broken! I choose to walk in divine health and healing daily! I oppose sickness in all its forms. I speak the Zoe life of God to every cell, tissue, organ, and system in my body. I declare that by the stripes of Jesus I was, and am healed. My salvation in Christ also included my deliverance, healing, restoration, and wholeness. I receive and appropriate them now. Spirit of infirmity, I bind you and declare that you have no place or authority in my life. I oppose, cancel, and reject heart disease, high cholesterol, cancer, high blood pressure, and every form of sickness from my life and body. I say NO to covid, infection, cold, flu, and allergies. I choose life, and declare that I walk in abundant life. No evil will conquer me; no disease will infect me, and no plague will come near my home. Jehovah Rophe is my divine health and healer. I am safe in Him.

___

___

___

___

___

___

___

___

___

___

___

___

___

I AM A FRIEND OF GOD

Scripture

I no longer call you slaves, because a master doesn't confide in his slaves. But I call you my most intimate and cherished friends since I have told you everything the Father told me – John 15:15.

Proclamation

I AM a friend of God! Jesus calls me His friend. When I was utterly helpless, Christ came at just the right time and died for me. Most people would not be willing to die for an upright person, but God showed his great love for me by sending Christ to die for me while I was still a sinner. I am a friend of God. My friendship with God was secured by the death of his Son, and now, I am saved through His life. I am not a friend of the world, because friendship with the world means enmity with God. I do not love the world, nor the things that are in it, because the love of the Father is in me. The world offers only a craving for physical pleasure, a craving for everything we see, and pride in our achievements and possessions. I say No to the world and Yes to God. I rejoice in my wonderful new relationship with God because my Lord Jesus Christ has made me a friend of God! Jesus is my friend that sticks closer than a brother.

AFTERWORD

Your identity and worth are intrinsic and rooted in your relationship with God. You have a purpose and destiny far greater than anything that happened to you. It doesn't matter what you have done or been through. You can begin again, TODAY. It's called redemption and His name is Jesus! God has a strategic move in your future that will restore all that you lost. God has anointed you to prosper and empowered you to succeed. He has kingdom connections and divine encounters all pre-arranged for you. You are on a collision course with destiny!

How can you accelerate your destiny and bring it into manifestation? By proclaiming the word of God; saying the same things about yourself that God says about you.

Your life and death are in the power of your tongue. Speak Life!

OTHER BOOKS BY THE AUTHOR

Choices That Make Or Break, LifeWork Press, 2022

W.H.O.L.E: 5 Practical Steps To Wholeness In Spirit, Soul, And Body, LifeWork Press, 2022

The Colt Story, LifeWork Press, 2021

I AM The God Kind, Living in the Reality of Your Identity in Christ, LifeWork Press, 2021

Fight to Win with Prayer and Proclamations, Grivante Press 2020.

Choosing a Life of Victory, Xulon Press 2019.

Single and Happy, Are You A W.H.O.L.E Single? Xulon Press 2019.

Single and Happy, Are You A W.H.O.L.E Single? Study Guide.

Workbook: 5 Practical Steps to Wholeness in Spirit, Soul, and Body.

AUTHOR MINISTRY RESOURCES

LIFEWORK MINISTRIES, INC.

LifeWork Ministries empowers people to live the abundant life in Christ. We preach, write, and witness! Our compelling mission is to release the Life of Christ into the world by using our faith, thinking our faith, speaking our faith, singing our faith, praying our faith and sharing our faith. Connect with us on our website: **www.lifeworkministries.org** or send us an email at **lifeworkministriesinc@gmail.com**

WEEKLY RADIO BROADCAST

Gloria has a weekly Bible teaching program on REACH Gospel Radio. You can hear her radio broadcast in cities across America. For the schedule of her weekly radio bible teaching program, please go to our website: **www.lifeworkministries.org.**

LICENSED CLINICAL PASTORAL COUNSELOR & TEMPERAMENT COUNSELOR

At LifeWork Ministries, we provide individual, family, marriage, pre-marital, relationship, career, ministry, and teen counseling. Contact us on our website at **www.lifeworkministries.org**

iDECLARE PRAYER AND PROCLAMATION

Gloria hosts the iDECLARE Prayer and Proclamation event. The word of God, spoken in faith, is the most powerful weapon known to man. At iDECLARE, we load, cock, and fire the word of God to transform our lives, families, and nations!

RACIAL EQUITY & UNITY

Gloria leads the Biblical Equity and Unity (BEU) collaborative, hosts the monthly BEU Community dialogue and the annual Racial Equity and Unity luncheon. Our vision is to educate, engage, and advocate on issues of biblical equity and unity; and to promote racial reconciliation and healing. Facebook@REUofDE.

SAVED SINGLES SUMMIT

Gloria hosts the Saved Singles Summit, a premier Christ-centered forum, which brings together Christian singles from churches across America for a time of fun, fellowship, empowerment, kingdom connections and new opportunities. Join us at: **www.savedsinglessummit.com**. Facebook@savedsinglessummit.

SINGLE CHRISTIANS CONNECT MEETUP GROUPS

For clean, fun, weekly activities and social events.
https://www.meetup.com/single-christians-connect/
https://www.meetup.com/philadelphia_single_Christians-connect/

SINGLE SENSE CONVERSATIONS

Monthly fun, interactive, Zoom panel discussion on singles issues, every 4th Friday.

THE GRACETALK

Weekly internet talk show hosted by Gloria on Sundays at 6pm:
https://www.facebook.com/TheGraceTalk/live_videos/

AUTHOR CONTACT:

lifeworkministriesinc@gmail.com

ABOUT THE AUTHOR

Gloria Godson is a multi-faceted corporate executive, with an illustrious career in the Energy Industry. She is a visionary, thought and strategy leader, and consummate senior executive. An attorney by training, she rose through several executive leadership positions to become a Vice President in Exelon Corporation, the largest energy company in America.

Most importantly, Gloria is a Christian leader, Bible teacher, author, prayer minister, and conference speaker. She is a Licensed Clinical Pastoral Counselor, Certified Temperament Counselor and Professional Clinical Member of the National Christian Counselors Association. She has a weekly Bible teaching radio program, and hosts "*The GraceTalk*", a live weekly internet talk show. Gloria hosts Wholeness Workshops, Temperament Workshops, the premier annual Saved Singles Summit, the iDECLARE Prayer and Proclamation event, and the Racial Equity and Unity Community Events.

Gloria served on the Board of Word of Life (WOL) Christian Center in Newark, Delaware, a full gospel, non-denominational church, for over twelve years. And for over fifteen years, Gloria also served as overseer of the WOL prayer ministries, and is a regular eye witness to God's miraculous answers to prayer. She is a powerful minister of the word of God, with a singular focus on building lives and the kingdom of God. She is a dynamic speaker who connects with both professional and Christian audiences across the country and around the world.

Gloria loves to serve her community! She is on the Board of Faith and Freedom Coalition Mid-Atlantic. She is also a dedicated volunteer with the REACH community outreach, the Sunday Breakfast Mission, Urban Promise, Exceptional Care for Children, Friendship House, and more.

Gloria loves God passionately and believes in the unstoppable power of Almighty God to do the impossible. She lives in Delaware, United States, with her family.

NOTES

www.ingramcontent.com/pod-product-compliance
Lightning Source LLC
LaVergne TN
LVHW041542070526
838199LV00046B/1793